The Uncommon Nativity of Common Things

This book is dedicated
to Fritz and Alex.

THE UNCOMMON NATIVITY OF COMMON THINGS

Poems by

Katharine Redfield Carle

Antrim House
Simsbury, Connecticut

Library of Congress Control Number: 2014960365

ISBN: 978-1-936482-81-8

First Edition, 2015

Book design by Rennie McQuilkin

Front cover illustration ("The Fish House")
after a watercolor by Scranton H. Redfield

Author photo ("There Will Be Time")
by Rennie McQuilkin

Antrim House
860.217.0023
AntrimHouse@comcast.net
www.AntrimHouseBooks.com
21 Goodrich Road, Simsbury, CT 06070

Thanks Be

to those who have been so supportive of my work and have often made valuable contributions: my family members; everyone, residents and staff, at Greater "Seabury Life" – especially Doris Armstrong, Joan Cox, Joy Floyd, Nancy Kline, Sarah McQuilkin, Carol Simpson, and members of the Seabury Poets and Writers Guild; my church family, especially the Reverend Patricia Hames and Barbara Campbell; the members of the Greater Hartford poetry community, especially John Stanizzi and Marilyn Johnston; and my editor and publisher, Rennie McQuilkin, the person without whom this book would not be. Dear readers: please know that if I tried to name all of you who have been important to me as a writer, I would surely hurt someone by omission.

I also thank the editors and publishers of my previous books, *Enter the Wood* and *Divided Eye*, as well as the editors of the following publications in which certain of my poems first appeared, often in earlier versions: *Common Ground Review; Helix Art and Literature Magazine; The Frost Place Anthology of Participant Readings; Theodate, a Poetry Journal;* and *Voices.*

Table of Contents

PRELUDE

I. FAMILIAL

II. THE ART OF LOVING

The Uncommon Nativity of Common Things

MAKING DO

They're words, used, discarded,
found in gutters and scrap heaps.
Pick them up, listen to what they say.

If they're rusty, polish them.
Bent? Straighten them.
Too big? Whittle them down.

Put them to work, fit them –
like parts of a puzzle – together.
And out of their jumble

there it is, the portrait
of that fly-away day
you thought had gone astray.

I AM

If all my poetry, my art,
were to be reduced
to one theme

it would be a shout
a reaching out
to you:
a verbal embrace.

Across this vast, empty landscape
two travelers spy
each other and cry,
"Here I am!"

I. FAMILIAL

I, MARTHA

I have found my beginnings
in a faded sepia document among my mother's belongings:

I Martha Ellen Cassino Porter of Salem, Massachusetts
gather together the facts I know
of my father, John Cassino
born in Genoa, Italy 'round about 1802.

His father died young. Giovanni hated
his mother's choice of another man
who, wooing and winning her, strapped on the sword
of Giovanni's father. First his dead father's uniform,
then his sword! Non! Intollerabile!

He hurled himself down the mountainside to Naples,
but not before he seized the cloth from under the wedding feast,
tore it from the table, upended the celebration. He was gone
in the clatter of the catastrophe.

A slight young man might slip unseen aboard
a ship making ready to sail from the quay.
Once out to sea what could they do but put him to work
en route to Scotland.

There, the Laird of Dundas Castle on the Firth of Forth
did everything but make him his heir.

At 22 Giovanni, now John, decided to seek his fortune
in America. He found my mother, Martha Grush,
and made her his bride. She bore him three children.

Life was good in Salem, Mass.
John was an impatient man and worked hard to make his mark.

The keeper of the vessel "Eclipse," one night he made
to shut up the ship before a storm should catch her with
hatches open and decks unsecured.
Tripping, he fell, the heavy hatch striking and knocking him
into the hold.

They carried him to his house nearby, laid him on his bed
and stood, hats in hand, waiting for the doctor.
He never came to.
By sundown next day he was dead.

It was 1834 and the short life of Giovanni Cassino was over.
But he'd left his son, John Trask
to produce my great grandfather, Samuel Edson Cassino
who begat Margherita Osborn
who begat Margherita Forbes Redfield, who begat me,
Katharine Redfield Carle.

THEN

Through five and six
I lived in my own world.
I had the smallest room of all. Its only window
looked out on a peaked roof, my grandmother's
quarters over the attached garage.
I'd climb out of my window and straddle
the roof ridge, in control.

Good days, I ran off
clothed only in boxer shorts and sneaks.
To live my life as Jungle Boy, I'd tear up
to the top of the street and plunge
into the Endless Forest with its wild
grape vines to swing on.
I'd play from morning 'til Dad came home at night.

Stormy days I built dams in the gutters
of rain water running down the streets.
I made lakes and sailed paper boats on them.

Nights I was Tinker Bell. I would circle the room
and fly out the window, swooping and diving,
at night's end swoop back in again,
scrape my back on the half open sash.
I bear the mark still, reminder of that other world.

46 HARTLEY

Under dirt and debris, a slab
I sweep clean.

Crouching before it I see a lichen-covered surface,
a hole at its center. I carefully
dust and watch some glyphs appear.

Mysterious, perhaps a leg, then two,
a beak – no, a rune, no,
they look like letters –
a *K,* an *R,* and something that may be a date.

Now it comes back.
His man's hand guiding mine,
we have pressed our initials into the wet cement
of a footer
on a warm November day: our first collaboration.
Now the date comes clean.

11/40. Seventy-three years
have passed since we put our heads together
in his basement realm of tools,
reading his diagram
for what the footer will help support.

Standing by my initials or his (they are the same)
we see the diagram come to life:
a flight of stairs and a landing
emerging out of the unoccupied air
as we inhale the wet mud odor

of lime, silica, and water,
savor the smell of wood new cut for stringers.

I am my Dad's helper, apprentice,
glowing in his approval. I am not yet the girl
he hoped would be a boy.

THE FISH HOUSE

1. ’38

It’s the summer of ’38, and the weather is great!
Dad’s just bought us three girls our own boat,
a second-hand dory. It takes the three of us
to pull it up on the beach above high water.

We take turns learning to row, grudging the others.
Sometimes we go ’round in slow circles. But
September is here too soon! We’re off to school
’til on a Wednesday, the 21st,

a giant wave bores in from the east and takes down
the wharf, the hotel, and our little shack, the Fish House.
If we’d been there, we would have been washed
like the roofs of the cottages, far inland.

No Fish House standing, except a splinter of post
jagged against the sky. Until the miracle:
the “boys” fill her footprint with a sister shack
from higher ground. Our childhood fun can go on!

2. Changing in the Fish House

When summer came again, swimming was
the first thing on my mind. Sand and water.
But there were rules.
Bigger girls could use the changing room first.
I, the "baby," had to change with Mom.

The new changing room was so cramped
with fishing rods, buoys and pails,
tools, nets, table and chairs crammed in
that it left scant space for Mom and me.

She was out of her clothes so quickly
that I was nose to nipple with her breasts,
those pendulous, brown-tipped, hair-decorated
things that portended all of the growing up
I wanted none of.

COLLECTING

Yet each man kills the thing he loves.
– Oscar Wilde, *Ballad of Reading Gaol*

Small hands hold a homemade
butterfly net – a mop handle, coat hanger
twisted into a circle, and a dime's worth
of cheese cloth netting.

The vacant lot across from the house is
the perfect meadow. Here are hornets,
darning needles, moths, bees,
AND butterflies.

With no subtlety, I swipe a black-edged Monarch
and he's mine! Back at the house, in my cellar
laboratory, I open the jar of chloroform I'll use
to stabilize him. (That's what the druggist called it.)

I open the mayonnaise jar with cotton in the bottom,
then the small chemist's bottle of chloroform,
receive a whiff, momentarily intrigued
by its scent and power,

drop some swiftly into the mayo jar. Holding the net
above the jar, I let gravity and fumes work to
drift the Monarch down onto its
cotton bier. Soon he's out – stabilized.

AT YOGA

for Joy

We are air planing,
one leg planted,
one leg up, back,
and in the air.

Arms are out making our wings –
heads are up, looking forward
as the captain of his airship does.

I'm out again at Mix's pond
where the flag is up, the pond is frozen.
We've tramped miles, skates on shoulders,
to lace up and glide off on smoothed ice.

I'm gliding down wind
down the ice, lifting one skate,
holding its blade in my hand,
lifting it skyward, an aerial split.

A joy, an exulting
I can neither name nor
fully express
flies higher than I.

CHILDHOOD CAPER

for Alex

Our little tow-headed
run-away boy
has disappeared again.

From summer's steamy apartment,
down the front steps and out into the world
he stole away before anyone awoke,
clad only in his favorite shorts and boots,
shiny black pull-on-over-bare-feet boots.

Armed with a broom stick to unhook
the lock we'd placed too high for him,
he'd gone in search of adventure.

To the beach, where,
while the waves didn't catch him,
the police *did.*

When we arrived at the fire station,
our darling boy sat surrounded
by admiring officials, dwarfed by a
giant fireman's helmet, still bare-chested –
grinning, eating ice cream.

Oh God, please take care of this little guy!
May all his adventures end as happily,
may he grow up to be a thorn in the side of
grey people everywhere.

FAMILY REUNION

"Not at my table," she says,
asserting her authority on this,
the annual bumping of the generations
against each other.

My son has sat down to the holiday table
with his cap on. Always the cap.
A six gore with cupped visor,
it shades most of his upper face.
"In the 21st century, every one,"
he tells my sister, "wears caps."

She: "Show some respect!
I remember when men doffed their hats
if they met a woman on the sidewalk."

Now, humbled
by his public dressing down,
my son removes his cap,
reveals his naked crown.

WHAT I SAY

for Fritz

I hear his voice from 40,000 feet
over the bone-dry plains of Nevada
as he flies, not home, but
back to California.

He says in his restrained way
how hard it is, at sixty, to leave
his family.
His sense of the old,
the familiar has been renewed.

I want to say,
Put on the garment of intention,
let it cover the shirt of sorrow,
let this raiment protect you
from the occasional showers of doubt.

Like a miner going into the dark
may your head lamp be a beacon
that lights your way to your goal.

Don your mantle of calm
Tighten your core of peace about you.

What I say:

"I love you, dear."

"Thanks, Mom –
Love you back."

GRADUATION

for Alex

They had lined up two by two,
girl and boy, white and green. The girls
had been instructed to do that halting
slow step brides are taught to do with their Dads,
going down the aisle to the give-away.
In the smartest class the school has ever graduated
this reed of a mischievous brown-eyed scamp
who appraises you with her full-lipped calm regard
has received two scholarships.
She's distracted now, farewelling her friends
while her Dad, standing apart, weeps
silently, beautifully.

GRANDDAUGHTER

Dear child of my child,
where does this day find you?
What sky looks down on you?
I am bereft,
missing your humor, so smooth

like a polished apple.
I miss our conversations in French,
your tattoos, your letters
using every corner to say your love.

Where are you?
I know you need help.
All-y, all-y in free! Come in,
come in, wherever you are.

STEALING FROM MY SISTER

a toy or book when we were young,
a sweater or a dress in our teens,
never a boyfriend (she only had one).
Now I want to nick a picture
from our past, the family shack
on the shore,
and in addition, Patience, Toleration.

CARITAS

With a primordial ache I long for her
as we only do for the familiar
earth, trees and stones of family and home.

I'm visiting my sister.
I need to touch her – her intimate thoughts
and memories obscured from me.

I remember monkeys grooming each other,
sometimes mother and child, sometimes siblings –
I long to companion her like that.

I coo bird-like, lean forward,
lightly touch her on the arm, but it's a poor way
to read lost thoughts.

I yearn to be a monkey on a branch with her.
I'd sniff her scent, locate her itch, and scratch it.

VIGIL

"Dad, can you hear me?
If you can, squeeze my hand."

"Kappy, I've – had a – happy life
and I'm – proud of you.
You've been – a good daughter."

At the service,
Padre, old trekker with Dad,
likened his departure to the gleam
over the hills of New Hampshire
when the sun has sunk below,
casting a warm glow.

And I saw how his face warmed
with joy the day we set our
initials in the cement of the footer
we'd poured together.

THE LAST ACT

It was Thanksgiving Eve.
I was standing my watch.
I sang some lullabies
she used to sing to me.

Every once in a while I'd stop
and take her pulse.
Then I started to count
how many breaths a minute I took

and how many she. I took 15, 17 . . .
The more I counted, the more I took.
She took 6 or 4 . . .
I spoke into her ear, "Are you thirsty?"

The only response was a mouth open,
a thick tongue protruding. I rang.
"Can't we give her some water?"
"Only a moistened sponge

which you hold to her lips.
If she wants it, she'll suck on it."
I did this and she did. I thought
of another thirsting, another sponge.

I sang, I talked, I prayed,
I slipped away into sleep.
At four they woke me to say
my Mom had passed away.

GOODBYE

for Betsy Rich

Coming downstairs, I see
more than I want: the knot
of neighbors gathered,
the police car,
ambulance men approaching.

We three huddle to let them pass,
watch to see if they turn left or right
and find it's either Jack or Betsy.

Jack, beloved friend,
can't lift his right hand to his mouth,
has probably had a stroke.

When they wheel him out,
propped on a stretcher
between cardiac monitors,
medical hardware, he waves gaily
with his good hand
and calls out "Good byyyeeee!"

WEB

for Joan Sereda

Another of us is leaving.
How is it that she is still beautiful,
her blonde hair
the curls of a little child, her body
composed, a little child asleep?

Like the tremble of a web
what moves one moves all.
Other issues left behind,
we draw together.

PRAISE

Wrapping scarves over withered arms
we extend to touch each other –
we form the circle that has
no beginning, no end.

Like the dervishes whirling,
like David dancing before his Lord
or perhaps just like our own old selves,

we raise our arms,
lift weathered faces to earth's sun star
in the age-old ritual we share with all
creatures here below,
and offer our bodies as oblation.

The ground resounds
with the beat of our feet
as we turn our bodies slowly,
become the dance,
old bodies dancing new.

We are the circle that has
no beginning, no end.

FIGHTING WWII

We were fifty passengers on a bus
rolling through the flat German breadbasket,
between Gertwiller and Boxwiller, on a grey
Thanksgiving kind of day – looking for landmarks
that would take our husbands back to their war.

From the back came a shout: "We gotta get out.
Stop! This is where I got mine!"
Only a farmhouse and barn against monotonous terrain.

But we trooped off the bus and followed
to the back door of the farmhouse where we
surprised a French farmer having breakfast –
napkin 'round his neck, crumbs clinging to his mustache –
with a request to look into his barn.

In the barn we heard it all.
"With fire coming from the distant woods, we took cover
in this barn. Before dawn the door opened;
we thought it was one of us come back from taking a leak.
It was the Bosch. They killed the two guys
next to me, wounded me in the leg, would have killed me too
but one of our guys returned fire and two Germans
fell square on top of me, knocked me out, but hid me.
When I came to, none-a-you guys was there. I found a rake

for a cane and staggered out, but you had all gone.
You guys deserted me!"

Silence as we mounted the bus. Underway,
the unit's colonel came up the aisle:
"We didn't desert you, son. We came back twice to
find you – no luck, and headquarters ordered us to move out."

Embraces, tears. Next day, his wife searched me out to say
it was the first night he'd slept soundly.

THE NURSE

for Doris

"All I ever wanted was to be a nurse,"
she muses as she assesses my hurt.
"Oh, and to travel."

Now she washes her hands, now
she carefully parts the hair to better
see the field, and now I know why
she is the nurse she is.

Deft fingers ever so gentle
probe the area, read the skin
for signs of swelling, pain, infection.
Responding to her healing touch,
my swollen skull calms.

She is always who she sometimes is,
walking toward a problem, or a patient,
her manner a bulwark against
the chaos of crisis.

Only rarely a flare of anger
when we're slow or sloppy,
then reflection and repentance –
she's calm again.

And like the round of my scalp,
the world is calmer for her presence.

SONG OF THE LOZENGE LADY

I am so sorry
I can't rush up to you
with my last cough drop
to save you from a possibly
fatal coughing spasm,
because I don't have a cough drop
and you don't have a cough.
But if you did have a cough
and if I did have a cough drop
I would save your life.

II. THE ART OF LOVING

GRADUS AD PARNASSUM

for Valeshka

You are graduating,
graduating…

Repeat this word
in casual conversation
to passersby, to friends.
Graduation – a measure
of completion
or commencement?

What have you finished,
to what will you be promoted?

What do we do when
we step out from the world
of lessons and plans
made for us by the Other
to a world we must make
for ourselves?

Is graduating when
they call your name
and you know
you've grown to fit it?

HER RITE

Oughts
parade through her mind
like stiff little soldiers
prodding her with fixed
bayonets

to open her eyes,
bounce from bed,
head for Eureka,
ejected by some pneumatic
blast of energy.

But today she stops,
tells the boss
in the office of her brain

There are other things
I'd rather suck up.

She sets out the coffee
things: beans to grind,
milk to foam
for Kenyan Cappuccino.

On the table,
some open books of poetry.

Cup filled to its brim,
she sips and treats herself
to the uncommon nativity
of common things.

FOR ELEANOR

I dust once a summer, when Eleanor comes.

When my husband gently asks if the cobwebs
will make a permanent home for spiders, I say
"Just before Eleanor comes,
I'll give the house a good cleaning."

Or when I see the mould creeping
insidiously across the bathroom baseboards
I'm tempted to grab some cleanser and whisk it off
there and then, except I know that when Eleanor comes
I must have the house smelling sweet,
so I promise myself not to forget the baseboards
when I clean – before Eleanor comes.

As for the too-good-to-be-discarded closet relics,
they too must go –
like that great flare gun we bought for the sailboat
we sold in '86; maybe we could shoot off its flares,
make folks think they've seen a meteor shower,

just before Eleanor comes.

IF I WERE A COUNTRY

I'd want to be healthy –
all of me.

I wouldn't be at war with me;
each part would do its job.

I'd want a balance, an equity
between each part and system.

Fair weather for my upper part
wouldn't cause foul for the nether.

Food for my bread basket wouldn't
starve my soul or my brainy bean.

I wouldn't cut off my left hand
to please my right

nor favor my fairer regions
over the darker.

I want to be healthy –
all of me.

THE ART OF LOVING

Don't know when I began
to love my body.

Was it when I first noticed the web
of purple spiders on my legs,

or when I caught a senile keratosis
(my doctor called it) on my cheek,

or when breast tightening exercises
did nothing to prevent The Sag?

I shall not catalog further the desperate
measures my body has taken.

She's like a mother you've parked in
an old folks' home, far too busy for her.

She's feeling deserted. No one
to file her nails, hair left lank for days.

In tears, I turn to her, reaffirm my love,
promise to shower time on her.

I honor her now, anoint her rough skin,
pamper her with Pears, Crème Radiance.

UNDER THE INFLUENCE

Registration please . . .

First, walk nine steps heel to toe
in a straight line without falling.

Next stand on one foot 30 seconds.
Follow the moving finger.

Most can't perform these tasks
dead sober.

And why should we be
serious, sensible, and solemn?

We live in an intoxicating world.

STORM FEVER

I tell you I feel wild,
driving into a cloud that even at midnight
blackens the dark sky
rent by jagged slashes of lightning
so intense the blue-white scars remain.

I drive straight toward them, feeling
the hair rising on my limbs.
Oh I'm scared all right.
Suppose you're killed;
you haven't changed your will.
Better go back!
But I'm also tight with the storm
doing 60 on a country back road.

It goes silent; now, the shock
splits the air…
When I can see and hear again

I slip off my safety belt.
Better to drive back beeping
than be found fried on the highway.

I'm beside myself
with excitement. I gun the car.

As I reach home, the first giant drops
splatter themselves on my windshield;
I open the door, lift my face,
drink in the storm.

WINTER SPARE

It's New England spare with winter's onset,
I think as I'm driving over that same road
I drove last summer when the clouds
threatened and jagged lightning accelerated
me into the storm as fast as it came at me.

Now out of the grey comes a whirlwind,
snow driven horizontally by the incoming front.
On the cliffs across the fields
outlines of pines are blurred by this
sudden blast of white – and now it's gone.

This is New England tidied for winter's long haul.
This is fields bare, only corn stalks standing.
This is trees bare of leaves,
making us more visible,
more vulnerable.

It makes a virtue of the patience we'll need,
waiting for love to spring again.

THE TOKONOMA

According to Mrs. Miniver, the proper
answer to the end of the world would
be a good cup of tea.

At the entrance to the tearoom
in a *tokonoma* niche
under the hanging scroll and next
to exquisite tea bowls with their
script in ancient Japanese,

this one fire-colored flower,
its petals tinged with tongues of flame,
colored tips becoming more and more
delicate as I trace them to their center,
the yet unfolded center: mystery

as in the ceremony
of the sipping of the tea.

WHEN

When I am old
I shall choose to take my tea
in my mother's gold-rimmed
white bone china, poured
from her Royal Albert teapot.
I shall spread a small white
napkin on my lap
and "play lady."
But for now it's all chianti.

EIGHTY-FIVE

I enjoy being old (I think)
or at least I do right now.
I like telling folks
"In my 85 years . . ."
like a kid saying "I'm (almost) thirteen."
I've been claiming it a while,
trying it on,
having been in my 85th all year long.
As the mother of the new Self
I've been getting ready to birth,
I've been practicing my new identity.
What and who shall I be?
Shall I be outrageous,
sensible, dignified?
Oh yes, now I remember!
All those I've already tried.
Think, think! What to do?
Be my self, that's certainly new.

HEAT WAVE

Life's a lot like summer,
takes a long time to arrive
flowers exotic and brief,

marked by a long slow decline
punctuated by mild periods,
remarkable for its late season heat wave.

THE SENIOR GAMES

I am sporting my gold medal
after the polo pool battle.

I growled like a beast, bared my teeth,
grappled with Mary Ann for the ball,
beat it out of her hands, screaming
"Mine! Mine!" I think she let go in surprise.

I've spent 81 years trying to
become a lady. (The first four
don't count – when I went naked, etc.)

I was five when I bit my mother's
college roommate in her leg,
told her "I don't yike compady."
I don't remember this. They tell
that story often, and until today
I've been trying to do better.

I WANT

I want a perfect glass of golden
Chardonnay in elegant crystal.

I want it so cold and so excellent
it doesn't need ice.

I want to eat and eat and eat.
I want to feel bubbles

of happiness rise in my head
to banish the undone "musts."

I do not want
to bemoan my be-moaning.

I want to heave up
the negatives crawling inside.

I want to be younger again,
and somewhere else!

NOW

I'm traveling to the edge,
where water laps sand
at the end of this land –
to blue water.

I wade in, immersing my self
in water which smells
of the greater ocean beyond.
Smoothly I swim the harbor
to where, with fish-eye view
I spy a boat moored,
the sails ready to be raised,
anchor poised at the bow,

Relaxed, unafraid,
I'm ready – now.

III. IN WILDNESS

APRIL FOOLS

April 1st and no fooling,
it's snowing, blatantly white,
steadily. It's not this soundless
spectacle that wakes me but
the strident quack of ducks.

They're back!
Come snow, come blizzard
these mallards return
to our modest pond.
Out of the sky they drop,

he fully dressed in mating plumage,
greeny gleaming helmet of a head,
white circlet 'round his neck, black tail curl.
She, demure in her mottled brown,
defers to him. He claims his turf,
drives off a foolishly hopeful male.

Oh, let us too be fools for April,
Let us make poems on this wintry day
to her showers and flowers.

STAR SYMPHONY

A crescent moon is rising
with Jupiter above,
Venus bright below,
the atmosphere so clear
I have a vision of how the world
must have looked
before a single fire had been lit.
I smell the moon shining,
hear the sound of star light,
feel the heat of the music,
become a song myself.

ZEALAND

for Fritz

Deceptively easy,
bordered by July's grasses,
hobblebush, Indian Paintbrush,
the trail leaves the parking lot
meandering off toward distant firs

which provide shade and shelter,
though not from invisible gnats
in search of human scent.
Sweat soaks my shirt,
mats my hair;
I'm a feast for no-see-ums.

Birds sing all around,
invisible, like the gnats.
Trudge up, over tree roots,
along trails packed by native feet.

Hearing a new sound, distant river
running, homing in on the source,
I divert over mossy stumps,
by Indian Pipe in boggy patches
to my first view of the mountain stream,

Zealand River, where a few cautious
hops from shore
bring me to a mid-river perch
where a flat sheet of pink granite

spreads like a table
from which I cool my feet in rushing water
eager to join the Ammonoosuc River.

Press on refreshed. The last hundred yards
go steeply up giant, jagged rocks
until just above me
I see the underside of Zealand hut.

My son hauls me up
the last few feet to the porch.
(Fifty years ago I bounded up.)

A vast sea of tree tops spreads before me –
the Notch and Pemigawassett Wilderness
within a giant horseshoe old-men-mountains make,
the afternoon dressing them in greys and pearls.

They embrace me, welcome me back.
Lulled by the music of nearby falls,
I'm home once more.

YOSEMITE

In the treads of my shoes, Yosemite soil,
Yosemite's forest needles in my pockets,
shreds of Yosemite Sequoia in my hair.

Voices of the Awahneechee chant in me
of Tis-sa-ack, tall split rock,
Face of a Young Woman Stained with Tears

whose vertical, lichen-stained face opposes
lion-bodied, square-topped Totokonoolah,
the Great Chief, El Capitan – Yosemite spirits.

Taking them in,
my heart is opened
to the Sequoia, Santos of the high forest.

The spirit of the Valley,
the song it sings – *All things connected* –
makes my spirit free.

FINDING THE RABBIT'S HOLE

I must go down to the woods again,
to the lovely woods and the sky
and all I ask is a full sun
and a path to guide me by.

I must check on the birds,
make sure that they're fed,
see that there's grass for them
to make a bed,

find me the rabbit's hole,
the spot in the brambles where
the homely little vole
beds down with the hare. There,

a clutch of old berries that cling
to a cane
will fall to the ground
at the season's change.

They're wizened, they're dark,
but on tasting one, I
find a bitter-sweetness
with which I see eye to eye.

The moral of this story is:
some things old can be delicious.

RIDDLE

On the eve of the autumnal equinox
before the rise of a full pumpkin moon,
walking home I see a rich green leaf
flutter down in front of me,
crossing my path to land ahead.

Such a color in early autumn
as brings spring to the mind's eye
should make one suspicious.
I sidle up to it. Praying Mantis?
This road's no place for her.
I make to pick up what's a leaf again.

Nothing moves – except an eye
looking at me. Her cleverly hidden legs
appear from under her leafy back, but
she doesn't move, thinks to fool me still,
then lifts her leafy self and sails,
a leaf with a will, calls *katydid katydid* . . .

THRESHING IS

a form of thrashing, or so I found
when I was invited to a quinoa threshing party.
Should one be wary when invited to a party whose name
has "ing" at its end?

Quinoa is the smallest seed around.
There are orchid seeds the size of dust,
but they don't really count –
you can't eat 'em.

The trick is to, you guessed it – separate
wheat from chaff. There was so much more
chaff than seed that in the first fifteen minutes
I liberated ten seeds; they were protected by dark,

unlovely flower bunches that scratched the hands.
Thus the gloves. If a quinoa seed
isn't smaller than a mustard seed,
you can't prove it by me.

If you have faith even as small as a mustard seed,
you can say to this mountain, "Move from here to there,"
so Christ said. I couldn't even move the seeds
from the chaff to the bowl. And there we have it –

a Biblical lesson in how difficult it is
to remove the mote from your own eye!

FIRE

From our days in the cave
when fire was life-giver,
heat to warm us, flame
to cook our food,

it's become a convenience:
we click on the gas fireplace,
turn on candles.

Still, in some lonely countryside
in the dark of morning twilight
someone rolls from his bed,
makes his way to the hearth,

feeds last night's grave of coals
with a clutch of tinder,
brings the outdoors in
by opening doors,

throwing open the sash
to let the fire breathe.
He blows on the coals, creates
the first fire.

IV. ADAGIO

BELOW THE MOUNTAIN

after "The Great Wave at Kanagawa" by Karsushika Hokusai

Those foamed tips of the waves are talons
waiting to pluck the tiny oarsmen from their long boats
to appease Mother Sea.

Yet the sun shines, the foam glistens in its light,
and old Fuji sits serene – overlooks all human endeavor,
guards its cone with ever-present snow.

And we in our boats
below the wave that is always rising over us,
below the mountain, the deep of the sky – we are sized up,
sized down. We submit, submit, struggle on.

FISHING BOATS
LEAVING THE HARBOR

after Claude Monet's "Fishing Boats at Sea"

Three boats on a greener than blue sea
exit the harbor in an early morning haze,
each leaving her shadow behind her,
the slight chop in their wakes
the only disturbance on this glassy green.

Surely not much breeze
for the sheets of the lateen rigs are slack;
their mainsails are luffing.
Jibs on the forward masts are all but limp.

Morning fog disperses from both
sides of the scene. Sun reflects off a bank
of clouds on the near horizon
and splashes itself over the far-off sea
under a mauve, umber, cream and grey
sky. Mixed prediction for the day to come.

For all the gaiety of broad orange stripes,
these are working craft.
All seem at the ready to catch the wind,
all but one helmsman whose distraction
accounts for his boat's last place

in this small caravan.
That peculiar cast to the sky he sees,
heaviness of the moisture-laden air,
sun red at its rising – all bad signs.

Mated with his unease, he remembers
his whistle as he left her lying,
arms out to him after a night of love,
no turning back. He recalls the warning,
"Whistles rash bid tempests roar."

Just a little
wind, he thinks, *Mon Dieu, just a little.*

I, CELLO

She has pressed me to her breasts,
my left shoulder between them. She holds me

between her knees, her legs apart,
heels planted. Her hands flutter, white birds,

as she presses the strings of me,
plucks, caresses, slides her bow on them

to create the sounds that thrill through her –
the bass chords and rich minor melodies.

Her fingers tremble me to vibrato
and now she flies into allegro molto vivace.

She beats, slaps me
near the bridge to a sound so surprising

the vibrations I send through her return
to me, intense beyond sustaining.

LOVE

And then, one clear note – rising,
rising to unreachable height,
a liquid tone, like rung crystal,
sound floating, staying
just where it started, not dying,
not fading – suspended.

IN CONCERT

Concert goers should be seated
by their height: the shortest in front
and by gradation those of increasing height
until in the back row, giants

the size of the man who sits in front of me
now, who by his massive bulk obliterates
the entire orchestra, except for the little
Asian violinist in the right outfield.

And now she disappears as well
when the mountainous man shifts in his chair
and three rows move in unison.

He's deaf in his left ear
and he's affixed his enormous hand
to his right one, leaving only a small triangle
of space between chin and shoulder

through which I think I see – yes, it is Yo Yo Ma.
Oops, now he's gone again.

DRESSING THE POPE

It is decreed: the color of the Holy Spirit
is red. When the Pope bestows it
to save or bless, let him be dressed in the finest
red silk (from Baker Liturgical of Southington).

When the Pope is in his underwear
is he still a Pope? In his night shirt
can he contain
the Holy Spirit?

In his sottana and sash,
from his zuchetto to his pantofole,
wrapped in his mozzetta,
he goes forth each day.

But catch him without miter or stole,
cope or alb, is he still the Pope?
Who is this man in bed, brushing teeth,
eating breakfast? Can he expunge a sin?

We poets and prophets of our world
who, like priests, derive our power
from the Word – we too
depend on decoration for authenticity.

Who are we at the open mic without disguise?
We cover our aging shells with glitter,
adorn them with beads and jewels.
Or would black make us more genuine?

How sad we all go naked to eternity.

THE CRAFTSMAN

for Jeff

Grey and worn, it's been lying on the coffee table for years
since my neighbor gave it to me – some twenty years now.
I've not paid much attention to it. Redwood, I suppose.
"Driftwood," she said. "Found it on the beach north of Golden
Gate Bridge across the Bay, wild and deserted. Must have
floated there from up the coast where the redwoods are."

Now he wants to know if I would mind his borrowing it
to clean it up, stabilize its weaker branches,
polish it with Tung Oil and the sweat of his hands,
discover what the living wood says, or is, or wants to be.

This master craftsman is himself being shaped:
broken almost beyond repair, he is emerging from surgeries,
not just put back together, but re-aligned.
He is feeling his way along, just as now he'll search the wood
with his good right hand, check for weathering, rot,
undiscovered wounds.

He says he'll clean it, debride it, discover its vascular system,
just as his surgeon will when he restores this carver's hand
before it loses its touch.

REDWOOD

In the winter of a west coast year,
when great storms sweep in from the Pacific,
we drop our cones which hold their seeds.
Drying, the cone scales separate
and the seeds drop out.

Such a seed was I, come to ground
near the California coast. Nurtured
by the soil of trees fallen for centuries,
fog kept me moist while I grew.

Springing from earth I became a seedling
in a great redwood forest.
I drank of the sky's waters.
I grew tall and strong, an arm of a stalwart tree.

A fierce storm separated me from my trunk;
its mighty wind hurled me into a stream
where I rode the torrent down to San Francisco Bay.

Found on the rocky shore by a traveler from the East,
I was retrieved,
lay, grey and quiet, waiting.

Now in the hands of the craftsman
I am spirit; from the sun's fire

I am made spirit.

INNOCENT

In the Craftsman's cellar workshop
neatly laid out are the bits, burrs, buffers he uses
to smooth, sand, debride a stump or branch
he chances upon in his walks,
and in one corner "Innocent Observance,"
a huge section of bark from a singular tree,
at the heart of it a figure with a history of disaster.

Come late to church, a young man named Innocent
was in time to watch helplessly
as his church, 650 women and children locked inside,
was burned to the ground. Those who tried to escape
were hacked to death by Hutus.

A small tree next to the church had been charred.
Innocent pulled it up by its roots and fled to the hillside.
Shocked into insensibility,
he neither ate nor drank for two days.
When he regained himself, in his hands was a Christ
carved from the wood of the tree.

A traveler returning brought this directly to the Craftsman.
She told how Innocent had given it to her:

"I can't have it here; each time I hold it
I hear the screams unbearably.
Take it to America,
let them see,
let them hear."

The Craftsman mounted the Christ
on his large vee of bark in the shape of Africa
ascending, swirling like a whirlwind of fire.
The Christ nestles in the rift at its heart.

The twinning of two woods – dark char figure
against the lighter inner bark of this other tree –
tells of fire as destroyer and creator.

Human in agony, pain twisting the length of his face,
He stretches his arms upward
and outward, both in supplication and in blessing.
Forgive them, for they know not what they do.

V. IN THE SILENCE

STEP AWAY

Get this:
I'm in a prison.
I've never been in a prison
even to visit my grandson,

except that little one down south where
I went to take food to Roy, Elvira's husband
" 'cause they don' feed 'em there."

I don't know the routine – how you put your
stuff in a locker, how your arms must be covered.
No metal on your body (sets off the alarms in detectors).
Don't touch the inmates.
As if they were precious figurines in an exclusive shop,
not grey clad outcasts, treated "like they was nothin'."

All this in a rural Connecticut field and farm setting.
Tourists say, "How charming"
when they tour the barns and silos.
They don't pick out the rolls of barbed wire atop the fences.
They can't see the prisoners inside low buildings
where thousands spend their time and youth
like ants in a hill, busy, but anonymous.

I do it wrong. I ring the bell on the security machine.
I've forgotten to put my pocketbook in a locker,
and at the door to the visiting room, I set off something else.

"Step away from the door!"

says a trooper looking down at a quintessential
little old white-haired lady.
"What did I do?"
"STEP AWAY FROM THE DOOR!" he repeats
in a voice like a taser shock.

IN THE SILENCE

She'd sent Mary off that morning,
her cereal bowl still half full,
bow askew on her hair
as she flew out the door to
catch the bus, book bag bouncing
about her slight frame.

They'd had a tussle – she'd pouted
over the cereal,
hadn't finished her homework.

Mom relaxed and went back
to the kitchen to finish her coffee in the blessed
silence of the empty house.

At last! Time to do the Christmas shopping,
and none too soon. Mary was beginning
to snoop in the closets.

9:30 and ready to go!
She picked up the ringing phone reluctantly.

An official voice:
"Come to the school at once. There has been
an accident." No more. Caller gone. A prank?

A mile to school, but well before,
police cars by the dozens, flashing lights everywhere.
Car in the street, she runs toward the school

straight into the blocking figure of a burly
state trooper.

"Your name?"
"What's happened?"
"There's been an accident."
"Where's my Mary?"
"YOUR NAME!"
"Mary Cabot. Mary is my baby's name."

He turns to his list.
He turns away from her.
A terrible silence...

The silence will never be broken.

STOP AND SHOP

Mother or auntie,
she's generously made,
a canary yellow blouse
covering her full-breasted frame.

In her grocery cart
two kids yelling "Agin! Agin!"
as she whirls them in circles.

Round and round they go
with a larger child clinging
to the cart's outside
in excitement and terror –
"Do it agin!"

Until they catch sight of me,
the only white about,

and the whirling stops.
The smaller boy says, soberly,
"Makin' too much noise
gon' get us killed."

PIPER

"Diddle diddle dumpling,
Diddle diddle
Diddle diddle, diddle..."
is all she says – no, sings in a sandpaper voice,

a minute of a woman, brown, not an ounce
of fat, hair braided in neat rows
flat against her small head,
eyes hugely open, searching,
limbs bird-like bone, skin taut.

Here in Long-term Care
they call her Piper, this woman of no age.
"Diddle diddle dumpling,
Diddle diddle..."

At the table where they have seated her
an angry white brandishes a newspaper
to strike the young black woman
who brings her pills, cajoling her
in dulcet tones, like a brook over stones.

Piper sits straight, intensity itself,
every sinew engaged, rises up,
has new words, first time in months:
"We all goin' to the same place."

MEMORIAL DAY

Two red-as-fire engines, immaculately shined,
ladders pointing to a solid blue sky,
their chromes gleaming in the sun,
form an arch over the street.

A gigantic American flag is strung between them –
just enough breeze to make it flutter.
Drums, flutes, fifes and clarinets
materialize as high school marching bands.

Girl and boy scouts, color guards, bank tellers
march proudly down Main St. USA where we,
the black and white of us, wave small donated flags
with pride for our town and ourselves.

One truck, driven by a librarian, becomes a float,
Its sign says READ! your LIBRARY wants YOU.
Now the long line of vets from four wars, Humvees,
the town's EMTs . . .

Like our flag we're made of different colors, but
e pluribus unum: no one below, no one above.

EPHPHATHA

Be opened. Mark 7:34

“I forgot my water; going to buy one,”
I call, as our group settles in at a picnic table
while waiting for the ferry.
A woman at the next table looks up.
“No need,” she says, “I’ve got one here,”
reaching deep in the dark of her battered back pack.

She is an immense woman
with a face like risen dough, sweating heavily in a loose
thrift shop house dress.
I don’t want to take water from her.
It’s been in her back pack for God knows how long
with only He knows what.

She pulls out a full bottle of Poland Spring.
It looks good, has not been opened. Her smile
is radiant, and a light comes on. When I try to pay her
she protests, and we fall into conversation.

Her husband comes to fish, she says;
he has the day off from teaching in the Projects
where they live. We might be sisters, two old gals
away from home. It is good to drink this gift
of water from her.

DOWNTOWN CHURCH

In the 1840s brownstone church
the news is bad.
In the heart of a neglected downtown,
it has been a splendid Episcopalian cathedral,
but the city is now empty of people.

This August service is sparsely attended
and those in pews stand out
for the distance around them.

At the postlude when the organ
thunders with joy
for the end of the service,
a child tears past me in a buttercup dress,
dark hair streaming after,
runs pell mell up the center aisle
and altar stairs, to the organ.

She's the image of concentration,
crouched down near the pedal keyboard,
her chin cupped in her hands.
She wants to know how everything works.
We unite in laughter and hope,
the old and young, white and brown of us.

VI. STATIONS

SIMON

"You want me to what?" I said to the centurion
but he struck me on the chest, one mean blow
that pushed me back into the crowd, and I'm a big man.

He growled and grabbed the cross
from this poor bloody bastard
who didn't even have sandals, beaten so badly
he was disfigured, wearing just a loin cloth. And his head!
It was all matted with blood, mixed with unkempt hair
spiking up at all angles.

As you know, I had to go up to Jerusalem that day –
I had business on that street, the Street of the Oil Sellers.
I'd never seen so many people jammed into one stinking
alley – the cries of hawkers, lost children, din of hundreds,
slime of donkey dung, oils spilled, animal blood and vomit…

Well, they shoved this miserable beggar's cross on me.
I can't be looking out for everyone who's run afoul
of Roman law. Let him carry his own cross, for God's sake!

But where that street turned the corner, it got steep
going up the hill. He never would have made it,
so I took his cross and hauled it up,
though it bit into my shoulder, awkward unbalanced thing.
The man straightened, looked to the women following him,
crying and wailing.
He reached out with a tender touch to the older one.
Imagine!

Below the crest of the hill, I heard the ring
of steel on steel, and when I reached the Place of the Skull
a squad of Roman soldiers was busy nailing
two other prisoners to their crosses. Blood rimmed the spikes.

The soldiers were about to seize this man, when he laid
his hand on me. It felt light, like a dove.
He murmured some words I didn't understand,
though their sounds impressed themselves on me.

When they tore him from me and threw him to the ground,
I turned away.
Again I heard the ring of nails
but no sound – absolute silence from the man.

Then the crowd gasped with excitement; I looked around
to see the soldiers raising the crosses with the three men
nailed to them. I ran down the hill.
After all – I did have business.

Now, when I tell you of this, I still feel his touch on me,
still hear his words. Their meaning is beginning to come clear.

STATIONS

Campo Santo reads a sign at the covered entrance
to a path I follow, not knowing where it will lead.

Here, the California forest is drought-dry and 99°.
Many trees have died and the stream is dried up.

Passing under the entrance, I encounter
a small bronze figure bearing a crown of thorns.

The leaf-strewn way ascends beside a stream bed
that shows no signs of life. Along it, Jesus receives

his cross, He falls, Simon is made to carry the cross,
is changed, hears Jesus speak to the women.

The path becomes steeper, more rocky. Here,
Jesus is stripped, exposed. I climb harder, begin to sweat.

And now I see only His feet with nails through them,
hear him surrender. I am breathing harder.

Almost at path's end, I cross a bridge to a wide flat rock,
a place for prayer. Manzanita and scrub oaks bow down.

The Christ, risen, stands free, arms out in blessing.

EPIPHANY

Two stories high,
neither man nor woman,
an angel
of muslin, taffeta and silk

rests in the narthex
of the church.

When the time comes
and the star shines over
the mother and child,

the angel
floats mid-air up the aisle,
its stern visage
leaning forward,
to take its place over the altar.

It towers to the gothic rafters.
We are struck dumb
by this God-with-us moment.

HOLY SMOKE

Now, down the aisle they come
forty strong, the choir
robed in white, with verger, crucifer,
and thurifer swinging his smoking censer.

Just as, when children, we played our yo-yos,
throwing them out underhand
with a flip of the wrist to bring them back,

so the tall, erect African-American man
censes the unwashed in ritual manner,
casting out the censer and guiding its return.
When he reaches my row, in recognition
of my delight, he lets out the chain and to my
exclamation, "Round the World!"
he executes a 360 and holy smokes us twice.

ALL MANNER OF THING

Sin is necessary, but all shall be well, and all shall be well, and all manner of thing shall be well.
Dame Julian of Norwich

A church is silent and peaceful;
soft candle glow warms the dark.
God is near.

A bomb explodes in a crowd,
legs and arms, brown and white,
all torn from their housings.
Why has He forsaken us?

Gentle is the sunrise –
strength from God knows where
supports us.
O taste and see that the Lord is good!

Kids in a school, safe in their classrooms
no longer. Hundreds restoring order
can't bring back the dead.
God, Show us that all will be well!

May I walk softly into a sunlit world,
feel its restoring warmth,
see divinity in a daisy's face.
Be my rock, my fortress.

AMOR

to be performed by choir and congregation

We know, we know
that God and the Spirit are with us.

We believe and can feel Christ's love.
Why then, do we shiver when the words
warn we have not life if we do not believe.

Let me be possessed by God.
May the Spirit seize me.

Many have heard him,
some have seen him.
But I have not.

When His voice is gone from us,
when the sight of Him is hidden,
bring your Son to us
that we may hear and believe.

Come back to us
like the songs of unseen
birds of the air
whose clear calls tell us

Ubi caritas et amor, Deus ibi est.

after 1 John 5:9-13

GENESIS

And God said, Let there be light: and there was light.

Genesis 1:3

I will it, I will it! You must have declared
as You willed light and life of every kind
to come forth. And You gave us free will.

Did You know how much trouble we'd be?

We raise our eyes, build cathedrals
with the architecture of Your light
which pulls us up to heaven, and always

we fall. Oh Lord, bless us,
capable of great evil and great good,
raise us up and make of us a light divine.

BIRTHRIGHT

It was Two Sparrows Day, God Knows
the Number of Hairs on Your Head
Day, His Mercy is Infinite Day.

Somewhere between the Gloria
and the Agnus Dei, a dawning
understanding...

Not loving myself, how could I love
others, even my children?
I had married out of fear.

My first child was conceived in ignorance;
the second, his father tried to abort
by pushing me down a flight of stairs.

Stubborn kid that he was
and in love with being, he refused
to be unseated. Love for him,

for Everyone, upwells in me,
reveals God's love
is truly infinite.

THE COMFORTER

The ultimate comfort
is falling into bed
as if into the arms of a friend.

We curl like children,
love a special pillow, a blankie,
bury our heads in the fragrant
scents of childhood breath.

Be it a pallet, or be it a king,
a pillowtop or without a spring,
it's our refuge, our hidey place
warm with our animal warmth.

In the end
we fall into our bed and into
the arms of the great Comforter.

AFTERWORD

The Fish House mentioned on pages 11-12 and referred to on page 20 was located in Madison, CT on West Wharf Road. It began as a "Sabbath Day House" on the Madison Green, a place for "outlying church families" on Sundays. Eventually, heat came to churches and the Redfield family transported two of these little one-room houses down to the Madison beach by the wharf where ships were built and where a fisherman in the family occupied the house closest to the water. My father's generation began the tradition of using the beach for recreation. My sisters and I relished weekend shore life and mourned the loss of the first Fish House to the Hurricane of '38. We cheered when the second, which had stood on higher ground a little above the beach, was moved to fit the footprint of its predecessor. As my generation aged, it was necessary to sell the tiny house and its beach-front land. Its owner, now the Madison Beach Hotel, has torn it down and built a towering structure in its place. "Fish" was part of the lives of so many people that I wanted to give it permanence by putting it on the book's cover.

Also wanting you to see the *objet d'art* created by Jeff Dugan from driftwood and mentioned on pages 65 and 66, I call your attention to the photograph on the back cover. Jeff's driftwood sculpture, which sits on the table in that photograph, is entitled "Solstice Flame."

The author fishing near the Fish House

Born in the vortex of the Great Depression, Katharine Redfield Carle grew up as a tomboy in New Haven, CT. Marrying early as a freshman at Wellesley College, she mothered two sons while working in cardiac research to help her husband through medical school. In her second marriage to a man she describes as "the good husband," she inherited two daughters. As owners of travel agencies with a focus on educational journeys for museums and schools, she and her husband traveled much of the world. A Christian and a Buddhist, she tries to practice the Zen proverb that urges us to "chop wood and carry water" as a way to achieve enlightenment, which for her occurs in the process of washing the dishes, writing the book, and trekking the fields. Katharine Carle's work has appeared in a number of literary journals; in the 2001 anthology produced at The Frost Place, where she was an invited participant in the Robert Frost Festival of Poetry; and in two books, *Enter the Wood* and *Divided Eye*. She leads a writing group at the Seabury Retirement Community in Bloomfield, Connecticut, where she also plans literary events. In 2014 she continued her life as a traveler with a visit to Yosemite National Park, where she became fascinated by the culture and spirit of the native people of that region.

This book is set in Garamond Premier Pro, which had its genesis in 1988 when type-designer Robert Slimbach visited the Plantin-Moretus Museum in Antwerp, Belgium, to study its collection of Claude Garamond's metal punches and typefaces. During the mid-fifteen hundreds, Garamond—a Parisian punch-cutter—produced a refined array of book types that combined an unprecedented degree of balance and elegance, for centuries standing as the pinnacle of beauty and practicality in type-founding. Slimbach has created an entirely new interpretation based on Garamond's designs and on compatible italics cut by Robert Granjon, Garamond's contemporary.

To order additional copies of this book
or other Antrim House titles, contact the publisher at

Antrim House
21 Goodrich Rd., Simsbury, CT 06070
860.217.0023, AntrimHouse@comcast.net
or the house website (www.AntrimHouseBooks.com).

•

On the house website
in addition to information on books
you will find sample poems, upcoming events,
and a "seminar room" featuring supplemental biography,
notes, images, poems, reviews, and
writing suggestions.